3/10

CHANUTE PUBLIC LIBRARY
111 North Lincoln
CHANUTE, KS 66720

Ocean Life

Coral Reef

By Lloyd G. Douglas

Children's Press®
A Division of Scholastic Inc.
New York / Toronto / London / Auckland / Sydney
Mexico City / New Delhi / Hong Kong
Danbury, Connecticut

Photo Credits: Cover © Casey and Astrid Witte Mahaney/Lonely Planet Images; p. 5 © Azure Computer and Photo Services/Animals Animals; p. 7 © Jeffrey L. Rotman/Corbis; p. 9 © James Watt/Animals Animals; pp. 11, 17, 19 © Stephen Frink/Corbis; p. 13 © Lawson Wood/Corbis; p. 15 © DiMaggio/Kalish/Corbis; p. 21 © Chris Newbert/Minden Pictures

Contributing Editor: Shira Laskin
Book Design: Elana Davidian

Library of Congress Cataloging-in-Publication Data

Douglas, Lloyd G.
   Coral reef / by Lloyd G. Douglas.
   p. cm. — (Ocean life)
   Includes index.
   ISBN 0-516-25026-4 (lib. bdg.) — ISBN 0-516-23739-X (pbk.)
   1. Corals—Juvenile literature. 2. Coral reefs and islands—Juvenile literature. I. Title.

QL377.C5D58 2005
578.77'89—dc22

CHANUTE PUBLIC LIBRARY
111 North Lincoln
CHANUTE, KS 66720

2004010116

Copyright © 2005 by Rosen Book Works, Inc. All rights reserved.
Published in 2005 by Children's Press, an imprint of Scholastic Library Publishing.
Published simultaneously in Canada.
Printed in the United States of America.

CHILDREN'S PRESS, and WELCOME BOOKS, and associated logos are trademarks and or registered trademarks of Scholastic Library Publishing. SCHOLASTIC and associated logos are trademarks and or registered trademarks of Scholastic Inc.

1 2 3 4 5 6 7 8 9 10 R 14 13 12 11 10 09 08 07 06 05

Contents

1. Coral Reefs — 4
2. Coral Polyps — 6
3. Swimming — 16
4. New Words — 22
5. To Find Out More — 23
6. Index — 24
7. About the Author — 24

Coral reefs are found in warm waters.

Coral reefs are made of **coral**.

Coral is made of small sea animals called **coral polyps**.

Many coral polyps living together form coral.

Coral can be many shapes and colors.

A coral reef is made up of different types of coral.

Many plants and fish live in coral reefs.

Crabs and **shrimp** also live in coral reefs.

Sea turtles eat the plants that grow on coral reefs.

Some people like to swim in coral reefs.

They can see the many plants and animals that live there.

People like to take pictures of coral reefs.

They use special cameras that work in the water.

Coral reefs are a beautiful part of ocean life.

New Words

coral (**kor**-uhl) a substance found underwater, made up of the skeletons of tiny sea creatures called coral polyps

coral polyps (**kor**-uhl **pol**-ips) small sea animals that form coral and have tubular bodies and a round mouth surrounded by tentacles

coral reefs (**kor**-uhl **reefs**) underwater structures made up of coral and other materials that have hardened into rock

crabs (**krabz**) animals that have hard shells, four pairs of legs, two claws, and live in the sea

sea turtles (**see tuhrt**-lz) animals with a hard outer shell and paddles for feet that live in the sea

shrimp (**shrimp**) small, edible shellfish that have a pair of claws and a long tail

To Find Out More

Books
Animals of the Coral Reef
by Lynn M. Stone
Rourke Publishing

Coral Reefs
by Susan Heinrichs Gray
Compass Point Books

Web Site
Coral Reef Animal Printouts—Enchanted Learning
http://www.enchantedlearning.com/biomes/coralreef/coralreef.shtml
Learn about coral reefs and print out pictures of the animals that live there on this informative Web site.

Index

animals, 6, 16

coral, 4, 6, 8
coral polyps, 6
crabs, 12

fish, 10

plants, 10, 14, 16

sea turtles, 14
shrimp, 12
swim, 16

About the Author
Lloyd G. Douglas writes children's books from his home near the Atlantic Ocean.

Content Consultant
Maria Casas, Marine Research Associate, Graduate School of Oceanography, University of Rhode Island

Reading Consultants
Kris Flynn, Coordinator, Small School District Literacy, The San Diego County Office of Education

Shelly Forys, Certified Reading Recovery Specialist, W.J. Zahnow Elementary School, Waterloo, IL

Paulette Mansell, Certified Reading Recovery Specialist, and Early Literacy Consultant, TX